GORDON RAMSAY

Fish and Shellfish

GORDON RAMSAY

Fish and Shellfish

Photography by Simon Wheeler

WEIDENFELD & NICOLSON

Gordon Ramsay

Gordon Ramsay is the chef and proprietor of one of London's most popular restaurants, Aubergine in Chelsea, which has been fully booked since the day it opened in October 1993, and which has recently been awarded its second Michelin star. He is also proprietor of L'Oranger in St James's, which earned its first Michelin star within a year of opening.

Fellow chefs from top restaurants voted him the AA Chef's Chef of the Year for 1996. One of his peers commented: 'Gordon continues to come up with innovative and exciting ideas which have had a massive influence on the eating habits of London.'

He has appeared on BBC-TV's *Food and Drink* and *Masterchef*, and his first book, *A Passion for Flavour*, was published in 1996.

Contents

THE BASICS

The sheer beauty of a fresh fish makes me want to do full justice to its flavour and texture and present it in the best way I can.

Introduction

There is no doubt about it, fish and seafood has grown greatly in popularity over the past few years. Fish can be familiar or exotic, depending on seasonal availability and your budget. All fish is quick to cook and easy to make into a healthy meal. I love cooking fish because the sheer variety of flavours, textures and colours provide me with a wonderful base for creativity, like an edible artist's palette.

The twelve recipes in this book represent a good sample of my style of 'piscine cuisine'. I've included dishes using popular fish such as salmon, cod, crab and mussels along with more gourmet-style brill, tuna and sea bass for special occasions.

If you are new to fish cookery, don't be put off by the fear of preparation. A good fish-monger will be only too pleased to demonstrate his filleting skills, removing heads, bones, skin and fins in a matter of moments. Just choose a good quiet time to talk to him.

MUSSEL AND SAFFRON SOUP

SERVES 4

3 tablespoons olive oil
½ yellow pepper, finely chopped
½ red pepper, finely chopped
2 shallots, finely chopped
2 small sticks of celery,
    finely chopped
good pinch of saffron strands
4 tablespoons dry white wine
1 kg/2 lb 4 oz fresh mussels,
    scrubbed and debearded
1 litre/1¾ pints fish stock
    (page 36)
salt and pepper
3 tablespoons cream
2 teaspoons chopped fresh
    tarragon

In a large saucepan, heat the oil, then add the peppers, shallots, celery and saffron. Cover and fry gently for about 10 minutes, shaking the pan occasionally.

Add the wine and cook uncovered for a minute or two, then stir in the mussels. Cover the pan and cook for 3–5 minutes or until all the mussels have opened. Any that haven't opened should be discarded. Lift out the mussels using a slotted spoon. Remove the mussels from their shells and set aside. Throw away the shells.

Add the stock to the saucepan and bring to the boil, cover and simmer for 10 minutes.

Reserve about 2 tablespoons of mussels for garnishing and add the rest to the stock. Season to taste and simmer for a further 5 minutes.

Blend the stock and mussels in a liquidizer or food processor, then pass through a sieve, rubbing the mussels through with the back of a ladle. Return to the pan, add the cream and reheat to just below boiling point. Taste and adjust the seasoning, then ladle into four warmed soup plates. Garnish with the reserved mussels and chopped tarragon and serve immediately.

Stay in the Mediterranean mood and follow the soup with a salade niçoise made with freshly grilled tuna. For pudding, try a French-style dark chocolate tart or thin slices of chocolate torte.

FRESH SHELLFISH SOUP

SERVES 4

150 g/5 oz fresh winkles

150 g/5 oz fresh cockles

150 g/5 oz fresh clams

2 tablespoons olive oil

1 shallot, chopped

1 stalk of lemongrass, peeled
    and chopped

bouquet garni of fresh thyme,
    parsley stalks and a bay leaf,
    tied together

2 tablespoons Noilly Prat or
    dry vermouth

600 ml/1 pint fish stock
    (page 36)

salt and pepper

3 large basil leaves

To garnish

1 small carrot, cut into thin
    sticks

½ small courgette, cut into
    thin sticks

3 tablespoons cooked or canned
    cannellini beans

Put the shellfish into a large saucepan with 1 tablespoon of the oil. Heat with the lid on for about 5 minutes, shaking the pan occasionally until the cockle and clam shells have opened. Any that haven't opened should be discarded. Strain into a small bowl and reserve the juices. Remove the flesh from the shells and set aside.

Add the remaining oil to the saucepan, add the shallot, lemongrass and bouquet garni and cook gently for 5 minutes or until softened.

Add the reserved shellfish juices, the vermouth and stock. Season to taste and bring to the boil, then simmer for 10 minutes.

Remove from the heat, add the basil leaves and leave to infuse for 10 minutes. Strain through a sieve into a bowl, discard the solids, then return the stock to the pan and add the shellfish flesh.

For the garnish, blanch the carrot and courgette sticks in boiling water for 1 minute, then drain and rinse under cold water.

To serve, add the blanched vegetables and the beans to the soup and return to a light boil. Taste and adjust the seasoning and serve immediately.

For a main course, serve a juicy grilled steak, chunky home-made chips and a creamy mushroom sauce. Complete the meal with a light chocolate mousse and a few fresh raspberries.

TIAN OF CRAB AND GUACAMOLE

SERVES 4

100 ml/3½ fl oz groundnut or
    sunflower oil
1 stalk of lemongrass, peeled
    and chopped
2 egg yolks
salt and pepper
200 g/7 oz prepared white
    crabmeat
½ Granny Smith apple, peeled
    and finely chopped
selection of salad leaves
1 tablespoon simple vinaigrette
    (page 37)

Guacamole
1 ripe avocado
2 teaspoons fresh lime juice
1 small spring onion, finely
    chopped
1 tomato, skinned, seeded and
    chopped
1 tablespoon chopped fresh
    coriander or parsley
pinch of ground cumin

Put the oil in a small saucepan, add the lemongrass and 50 ml/2 fl oz water and simmer for 5 minutes. Leave until cool, then strain the scented oil and water into a jug. Discard the lemongrass.

Whisk the egg yolks with a good pinch each of salt and pepper, then gradually trickle in the scented oil and water, whisking well until you have a thick mayonnaise. Alternatively, make the mayonnaise in a liquidizer or food processor. Set aside in the refrigerator.

Flake the crabmeat and mix with the apple and 1 tablespoon of the mayonnaise. Season well.

When nearly ready to serve, toss the salad leaves with the vinaigrette. Set aside while you make the guacamole. Peel, halve and stone the avocado, then mash the flesh with a fork to a chunky purée. Mix in the lime juice, onion, tomato, herbs, cumin and salt and pepper to taste. Spoon a quarter of the guacamole into a plain scone cutter in the centre of each of four dinner plates, then press the crab salad on top and lift off the cutter.

Arrange the dressed salad leaves around the edge. Stir the mayonnaise until it is smooth, then trail in a ribbon around the salad. Serve immediately.

Follow this pretty first course with noisettes of lamb and a gratin dauphinoise. Pudding could be a rich vanilla ice cream into which you have stirred some chopped prunes and Armagnac.

Tartare of two salmons

SERVES 4

100 g/3½ oz filleted very
    fresh salmon
100 g/3½ oz smoked salmon
1 shallot, finely chopped
½ teaspoon fresh lime juice
1 tablespoon chopped fresh
    chives
1 tablespoon crème fraîche
salt and pepper
½ cucumber, peeled
4 quails' eggs
sprigs of chervil

Chop the fresh and smoked salmon quite finely, then combine with the chopped shallot, lime juice, chives, crème fraîche and salt and pepper to taste. Set aside in the refrigerator.

Cut the peeled cucumber in half lengthways. Using a teaspoon, scoop out and discard the seeds. Slice the flesh thinly into half moons. Layer the cucumber in a colander, sprinkling the layers lightly with salt. Leave for 20 minutes, then rinse and pat dry.

Bring a small saucepan of water to the boil, gently lower in the eggs and cook for 2½ minutes after the water returns to the boil. Drain and plunge into cold water. Peel and set aside. The yolks should still be very slightly soft.

To serve, make a fan of the cucumber slices in the centre of four plates. Place a scone cutter on top and press in a quarter of the salmon mixture. Lift off the scone cutter and repeat with the remaining salmon tartare. Top each salmon mound with a quail's egg and a sprig of chervil.

Serve this light summery dish with a green leafy salad and walnut bread. Start the meal with a crisp tart filled with sliced tomatoes, shredded basil and olive oil. Round off with a salad of lightly poached summer fruits accompanied by crisp shortbread biscuits.

FRESH TUNA SALAD
with white radish and balsamic vinaigrette

SERVES 4

300 g/11 oz loin of fresh tuna,
    in one piece
juice of 1 lime
grated zest of 1 small orange
    and 1 lemon
1 teaspoon coriander seeds,
    lightly crushed
salt and pepper
1 large white radish (also sold
    as mooli or daikon)
2 tablespoons simple vinaigrette
    (page 37)
1 teaspoon lemon juice
selection of salad leaves

Balsamic vinaigrette
5 tablespoons olive oil
1 teaspoon Dijon mustard
1 tablespoon balsamic vinegar

Place the tuna loin in a food bag with the lime juice, orange and lemon zest, coriander seeds and ½ teaspoon salt. Rub well together, then leave to marinate in the refrigerator for 2 hours, turning the bag occasionally.

Remove the tuna, rinse in cold water and pat dry. Wrap in cling film to form a tight roll, then freeze for about 15 minutes to firm the flesh slightly.

Meanwhile, peel the white radish and slice very thinly, preferably on a mandolin. Toss the slices with the vinaigrette, lemon juice and salt.

Make the balsamic vinaigrette by whisking all the ingredients together. Season to taste.

Place small mounds of salad leaves in the centre of four dinner plates and arrange the dressed radish slices in a circle around the leaves.

Remove the tuna from the freezer, unwrap and cut into wafer-thin slices, using a very sharp long knife. Lay the tuna slices over the radish.

Whisk the balsamic vinaigrette and swirl in a ribbon around the tuna. Serve immediately.

This makes a good starter, to be followed by a main course of tagliatelle with a wild mushroom sauce flavoured with a trickle of truffle oil. For dessert, serve a selection of red berry fruits sprinkled with sugar and lightly browned under a hot grill accompanied by a Champagne sabayon sauce.

SALAD OF SCALLOPS
with truffle vinaigrette

SERVES 4

12 new potatoes
selection of salad leaves
2 tablespoons simple vinaigrette
   (page 37)
olive oil for frying
12 large fresh scallops, cleaned,
   corals discarded

Truffle vinaigrette
4 egg yolks
salt and pepper
250 ml/9 fl oz groundnut or
   sunflower oil
2 tablespoons truffle oil
2 tablespoons truffle essence
   (optional)
4 teaspoons white wine vinegar
2 teaspoons finely chopped fresh
   truffle

Boil the potatoes until just tender, about 12 minutes. Leave to cool slightly, then peel and slice. Set aside.

To make the truffle vinaigrette, blend the yolks, salt and pepper in a liquidizer or food processor until thick and pale. With the machine still running, slowly trickle in the groundnut oil until you have a creamy sauce. Trickle in the truffle oil, truffle essence, if using, and vinegar. If the texture is too thick, adjust with a little hot water. Transfer to a jug and stir in the chopped truffles.

Toss the salad leaves with the simple vinaigrette. Place small mounds in the centre of four dinner plates.

Heat a little olive in a frying pan and fry the potato slices, turning once or twice, until browned. Remove and keep warm.

Wipe out the pan with paper towels. Add a little more oil and heat until very hot, just below smoking point. Add the scallops and fry for about 2 minutes on each side, until just caramelized. Do not overcook: they should feel slightly springy. Season well.

Arrange the potatoes and scallops around the salad leaves, then trickle over the truffle vinaigrette. Serve immediately.

A main course of plain roast chicken, green beans and a light creamy sauce would be good after the scallop salad. For dessert, make a crème brulée flavoured with orange zest and serve with sliced strawberries.

Red mullet
with braised fennel and pesto sauce

SERVES 4

2 whole red mullets, about
    400 g/14 oz each
salt and pepper
good pinch of saffron strands
    (optional)
8 baby fennel bulbs or 2 small
    fennel bulbs
25 g/1 oz butter
3 tablespoons olive oil
200 ml/7 fl oz fish stock
    (page 36)
4 tablespoons pesto sauce,
    preferably homemade

Ask the fishmonger to fillet (but not skin) the mullets so you have four whole, neat fillets, about 100 g/3½ oz each. Score each skin side about three times. Season the fillets, crush over the saffron strands, if using, and rub into the skin. Set aside in the refrigerator while you prepare the fennel.

Trim the fennel, reserving any fronds. If not using baby fennel, cut into quarters, leaving the root intact. Heat the butter and 1 tablespoon of the oil in a deep frying pan and brown the fennel all over. Add 150 ml/5 fl oz of the fish stock, bring to the boil, season, cover and simmer gently for 15−20 minutes, until the stock has been absorbed and the fennel is tender. Keep warm in the pan.

Mix the remaining fish stock with the pesto sauce and heat gently.

Heat the remaining oil in a heavy-bottomed frying pan. When it is hot, add the fish fillets, skin side down, and fry for about 3 minutes. Season, turn carefully and cook for another 2 minutes or so.

To serve, divide the fennel between four warmed plates and arrange the mullet on top. Trickle the pesto sauce around the fish and garnish with any reserved fronds of fennel.

A salad of sliced artichoke bottoms, rocket leaves and shavings of Parmesan cheese could precede this main course. Finish the meal with a hot pistachio soufflé with scoops of rich chocolate ice cream.

FILLETS OF BRILL
with three mustard sauce

SERVES 4

4 fillets of brill (or halibut or cod),
    about 150 g/5 oz each,
    skinned
salt and pepper
4 small Little Gem lettuces
3 tablespoons olive oil
25 g/1 oz butter

Three mustard sauce

15 g/½ oz butter
3 shallots, finely sliced
200 ml/7 fl oz dry white wine
200 ml7 fl oz Noilly Prat or dry
    vermouth
400 m/14 fl oz fish stock
    (page 36)
300 ml /10 fl oz double cream
1 teaspoon each of Dijon,
    Pommery and honey
    mustards

To serve (optional)
250 g/9 oz fresh peas, broad
    beans or fine green beans

Trim the fish fillets to neat shapes, season and set aside.

To make the sauce, heat the butter in a saucepan, add the shallots and cook gently for about 12 minutes or until softened. Add the wine and Noilly Prat or vermouth and boil until reduced by two-thirds. Stir in the stock and boil again until reduced by half. Add the cream and simmer for 15 minutes, until the sauce has the consistency of thin cream. Strain through a sieve, return to the pan and season to taste.

Cut the lettuces in half, leaving the root intact. Heat 1 tablespoon of the oil and the butter in a frying pan and fry the lettuces for about 5 minutes, until lightly coloured. Add about 4 tablespoons water, season and cook for a further 5 minutes, until softened. Keep warm.

In a large nonstick frying pan, heat the remaining oil and fry the fish for 3 minutes on one side. Turn over carefully and cook for a further 2 minutes.

To serve, reheat the sauce and whisk in the three mustards. Arrange two lettuce halves on each of four warmed plates. Lay the fish on top and spoon over the sauce. Lightly boiled peas, broad beans or green beans are a good accompaniment.

If you like to make your own ravioli, start this meal with homemade salmon ravioli. Alternatively, toss freshly cooked pasta in a creamy smoked salmon sauce. And for pudding, how about a French lemon tart?

ESCALOPES OF SALMON
with tomato and cumin sauce

SERVES 4

2 large potatoes, about 500 g/
    1 lb 2 oz, peeled
4 tablespoons double cream
50 g/2 oz butter, diced
freshly grated nutmeg
salt and pepper
250 g/9 oz cherry tomatoes
5 tablespoons olive oil, plus
    extra for serving
½ teaspoon cumin seeds
2 courgettes
few sprigs of thyme
4 fresh salmon escalopes,
    about 150 g/5 oz each

To garnish (optional)
fresh basil leaves or baby
    spinach leaves, deep-fried

First make the potato purée. Boil the potatoes until tender, drain well and return to the pan over a low heat to dry them off. Mash the potatoes until smooth, then beat in 3 tablespoons of the cream, half the butter, and nutmeg, salt and pepper to taste. Set aside and keep warm.

To make the sauce, purée the tomatoes in a liquidizer or food processor, then pass through a sieve, rubbing through with the back of a ladle. Heat 1 tablespoon of the oil in a saucepan and fry the cumin seeds for 30 seconds. Stir in the tomato purée and simmer for about 10 minutes or until reduced by half. Beat in the remaining cream and butter, season and set aside.

If you like, run a cannelling tool down the skin of the courgettes to decorate. Slice the flesh thinly. Heat 2 tablespoons of the oil in a frying pan and sauté the courgette slices with the tips of the sprigs of thyme and a little salt and pepper for 2 minutes.

Heat the remaining 2 tablespoons of the oil in a nonstick frying pan. When hot, add the salmon and cook on one side until well browned, about 3 minutes. Turn carefully and cook the other side for 1−2 minutes. Season well and keep warm.

To serve, reheat the sauce and add a little extra olive oil to thin it slightly. Make a ring of courgette slices around each plate, spoon the potato purée in the centre and place a salmon escalope on top. Spoon over the sauce and garnish with deep-fried basil or spinach leaves.

Begin the meal with a homemade watercress soup, into which you can slip some fresh oysters to poach lightly just before serving. Finish with bread and butter pudding.

GRILLED SEA BASS
with sauce antiboise

SERVES 4

2 whole sea bass, about 500g/
   1 lb 2 oz each
1 tablespoon finely chopped
   fresh rosemary, plus extra
   sprigs to garnish
2 tablespoons olive oil
salt and pepper

Aubergine purée
1 aubergine
1 large garlic clove, crushed

Sauce antiboise
150 ml/5 fl oz olive oil
2 shallots, finely chopped
1 garlic clove, crushed
4 basil leaves
1 tablespoon fresh coriander
   leaves
1 tablespoon fresh tarragon
   leaves
325 g/12 oz fresh tomatoes,
   skinned, seeded and chopped
1 tablespoon lemon juice

Ask the fishmonger to scale and fillet (but not skin) the fish so you have four long fillets. Score the skin sides about three times, then rub in the chopped rosemary, oil and salt. Set aside in the refrigerator.

To make the aubergine purée, preheat the oven to 220°C/425°F/Gas Mark 7. Cut the aubergine in half lengthways, slash the flesh a few times and rub with the garlic and some salt. Sandwich together, wrap in foil and bake for 50 minutes or until the skins have shrivelled and the flesh is very soft. Scoop out the flesh and chop finely. If you like, you can cook the chopped flesh in a saucepan to reduce a little for a firmer texture. Season and set aside.

To make the sauce, heat the oil in a saucepan, add the shallots and garlic and cook over a low heat for about 5 minutes, until softened. Meanwhile, shred the herbs into thin strips. Add the chopped tomatoes to the oil, together with the herbs and lemon juice. Add salt and pepper, heat until just boiling, then set aside.

When ready to serve, heat the grill until red hot. Grill the fish, skin side up, for 3 minutes. Turn carefully and cook the other side for about 2 minutes. Reheat the sauce over a low heat. Spoon the aubergine purée in the centre of four warmed plates and lay a grilled fish fillet on top. Spoon the sauce around the fish. Garnish with small sprigs of rosemary.

For a starter, serve a light chicken liver parfait or pâté, with thin slices of brioche toast. Follow with a lightly chilled rice pudding made with cream, egg yolks and vanilla, and trickled with a purée of mangoes or prunes.

TRANCHE OF COD
with special parsley sauce

SERVES 4

4 cod fillets, about 125–150 g/
    4–5 oz each, skinned
about 2 tablespoons plain flour
salt and pepper
300 g/11 oz new potatoes,
    preferably Jersey Royals,
    scrubbed
25 g/1 oz butter
2 tablespoons olive oil

Parsley sauce
15 g /½ oz butter
3 shallots, finely chopped
200 ml/7 fl oz dry white wine
200 ml/7 fl oz Noilly Prat or dry
    vermouth
400 ml/14 fl oz fish stock
    (page 36)
300 ml/10 fl oz whipping cream
about 200 g/7 oz fresh parsley

To garnish
sprigs of flat-leaf parsley

Trim the cod fillets to neat rectangles. Toss in lightly seasoned flour and set aside in the refrigerator.

To make the sauce, heat the butter in a saucepan, add the shallots and cook over a low heat for about 12 minutes or until softened. Add the wine and Noilly Prat or vermouth and boil until reduced by two-thirds. Stir in the stock and boil again until reduced by half. Add the cream and simmer for 15 minutes, until the sauce has the consistency of thin cream. Strain through a sieve, return to the pan and season to taste.

Pick the stalks from the parsley and reserve. Blanch the leaves in boiling water for 4 minutes, then drain well. Squeeze dry in a clean tea towel or thick paper towels, then purée in a liquidizer or food processor. Stir into the sauce.

Cut the potatoes in half and boil with the parsley stalks in lightly salted water until just tender. Drain well, discard the parsley stalks, and return the potatoes to the pan with the butter and seasoning.

When ready to serve, heat the oil in a frying pan and fry the cod fillets for about 3 minutes on each side, turning carefully, until just cooked, then season to taste. Gently reheat the sauce. Spoon the potatoes in the centre of four warmed plates and place the cod on top. Spoon over the sauce. Garnish with flat-leaf parsley and serve immediately.

This updated version of a traditional recipe could follow a starter of creamy leek soup, with a tarte Tatin of Cox's apples for dessert.

DIAMONDS OF SOLE
with Gewürztraminer sauce

SERVES 4

4 fillets of sole (or lemon sole),
    about 100 g/3½ oz each,
    skinned
about 2 tablespoons plain flour
salt and pepper
50 g/2 oz butter
250 g/9 oz mixed wild
    mushrooms (chanterelles,
    shiitakes, ceps, pleurottes,
    blewits)
about 100 g/3½ oz baby
    spinach leaves
2 tablespoons olive oil
2 ripe, well-flavoured tomatoes,
    skinned, seeded and diced

Gewürztraminer sauce
15 g/½ oz butter
2 shallots, finely sliced
350 ml/12 fl oz Gewürztraminer
    wine
400 ml /14 fl oz fish stock
    (page 36)
300 ml/10 fl oz double cream

To garnish
fresh chervil

To make the sauce, heat the butter in a saucepan, add the shallots and cook over a low heat for about 12 minutes or until softened. Add the wine and boil until reduced by two-thirds. Stir in the stock and boil again until reduced by half. Add the cream and simmer for about 15 minutes, until the sauce has the consistency of thin cream. Strain through a sieve, return to the pan and season to taste. Set aside.

Cut each sole fillet into about six diamond shapes and toss lightly in seasoned flour. Set aside.

Heat half the butter in a frying pan. When hot, add the mushrooms and stir-fry for about 4 minutes. Transfer to a plate, and wipe out the pan with paper towels. Add the remaining butter to the pan and when hot, return the mushrooms to the pan and sauté again, together with the spinach leaves, tossing until wilted. Season and keep warm. (The second sautéing keeps the mushrooms dry).

Heat the oil in a large nonstick frying pan. When hot, add the fish and fry for about 2 minutes on each side, until browned. Reheat the sauce.

Spoon the mushrooms and spinach in the centre of four warmed plates and arrange the fish on top. Spoon around the outside. Sprinkle the diced tomatoes around the plate and garnish with chervil.

Begin with a salad of lightly poached leeks tossed with a little vinaigrette, or a leek terrine. For dessert, fill a crisp sweet pastry case with caramelized mangoes and serve with pineapple sorbet and a little cream.

The Basics

CHOOSING FISH

It goes without saying that all fish should be bought as fresh as possible. A good indication of this is that the flesh shouldn't smell too fishy. Really fresh fish should smell of the sea, or even slightly sweet. The bodies should be firm and the skin shiny, not slimy. Eyes should be bright, full and fresh, not dull and sunken.

The shellfish my fishmonger delivers are so fresh the shells need a firm hand to prise open and the flesh almost pulsates.

TRIMMING FISH

In the restaurant kitchen, we pay great attention to fish preparation. Filleting is carried out with razor-sharp knives so the flesh remains undamaged, smooth and silky. We pull out the tiny bones with pliers and tweezers.

If a fish, especially sea bass or red mullet, is to be pan-fried we leave on the skin, which cooks to a brilliant crispness. Small fish are left as whole fillets, larger ones are cut into either rectangular or round slices, 'tranches' (round ones are made using scone cutters). Then we wrap the tranches or fillets firmly in cling film and chill them until required, to help firm the flesh so it cooks neatly.

COOKING FISH

I tend to cook fish in one of three ways: steaming, poaching, or pan-frying followed by a short 'roasting' in a hot oven.

Fish to be steamed is wrapped in cling film to hold its shape, then placed in a steamer over gently boiling water.

Fillets are gently poached in a court bouillon, a light fragrant stock of vegetables, herbs, lemon slices and white wine.

The simplest method is pan-frying. To do this at home, first preheat the oven to 200°C/400°F/Gas Mark 6. Heat a heavy-bottomed pan that is also ovenproof, until you can feel a good steady heat rising when you hold your hand over the pan. Add about 1 tablespoon of good olive oil, heat briefly, then place the fish in the pan, skin side down, and cook for about 3 minutes until the skin is crisp and caramelized. Place the pan in the hot oven, without turning the fish, to finish cooking for about 3–5 minutes, depending on the thickness of the fillet. If you don't want to use the oven, you can turn the fish carefully in the pan, using a fish slice so you don't break it up or tear the skin. Season the fish with sea salt and pepper while it is cooking.

FISH STOCK

MAKES ABOUT 2 LITRES/3½ PINTS

6 tablespoons olive oil
1 small leek
1 small onion
1 stick of celery
½ small fennel bulb
2 garlic cloves, unpeeled
about 1.5 kg/3 lb white fish
    bones or carcasses (eyes
    and gills removed)
300 ml/10 fl oz dry white wine
bouquet garni of fresh thyme,
    parsley stalks and a bay leaf,
    tied together
½ lemon, sliced
¼ teaspoon black peppercorns

Heat the oil in a large saucepan, add the leek, onion, celery, fennel and garlic and cook over a low heat for 7–10 minutes or until softened but not coloured.

Add the fish bones and wine and cook until evaporated, then add 2 litres/3½ pints water and slowly bring to the boil. Using a slotted spoon, skim off any scum that rises to the surface, then add the bouquet garni, lemon and peppercorns. Simmer for 20 minutes, then remove the pan from the heat and leave to stand for 10 minutes.

Strain carefully through a muslin-lined sieve. Leave to cool, then chill or freeze until required.

SIMPLE VINAIGRETTE

MAKES ABOUT 300 ML/10 FL OZ

50 ml/2 fl oz sherry vinegar
250 ml/8 fl oz extra virgin olive oil
50 ml/2 fl oz groundnut oil
juice of ½ lemon
sea salt and ground white pepper

Simply whisk or shake everything together until emulsified. Store in the refrigerator in a screw-topped jar and shake again before serving.

Classic Cooking

STARTERS
Jean Christophe Novelli Chef/patron of Maison Novelli, which opened in London to great acclaim in 1996. He previously worked at the Four Seasons restaurant, London.

VEGETABLE SOUPS
Elisabeth Luard Cookery writer for the *Sunday Telegraph Magazine* and author of *European Peasant Food* and *European Festival Food*, which won a Glenfiddich Award.

GOURMET SALADS
Sonia Stevenson The first woman chef in the UK to be awarded a Michelin star, at the Horn of Plenty in Devon. Author of *The Magic of Saucery* and *Fresh Ways with Fish*.

FISH AND SHELLFISH
Gordon Ramsay Chef/proprietor of one of London's most popular restaurants, Aubergine, recently awarded its second Michelin star. He is the author of *A Passion for Flavour*.

CHICKEN, DUCK AND GAME
Nick Nairn Chef/patron of Braeval restaurant near Aberfoyle in Scotland, whose BBC-TV series *Wild Harvest* was last summer's most successful cookery series, accompanied by a book.

LIVERS, SWEETBREADS AND KIDNEYS
Simon Hopkinson Former chef/patron at London's Bibendum restaurant, columnist and author of *Roast Chicken and Other Stories* and the forthcoming *The Prawn Cocktail Years*.

VEGETARIAN
Rosamond Richardson Author of several vegetarian titles, including *The Great Green Gourmet* and *Food from Green Places*. She has also appeared on television.

PASTA
Joy Davies One of the creators of *BBC Good Food Magazine*, she has been food editor of *She, Woman* and *Options* and written for the *Guardian*, *Daily Telegraph* and *Harpers & Queen*.

CHEESE DISHES
Rose Elliot The UK's most successful vegetarian cookery writer and author of many books, including *Not Just a Load of Old Lentils* and *The Classic Vegetarian Cookbook*.

POTATO DISHES
Patrick McDonald Author of the forthcoming *Simply Good Food* and Harvey Nichols' food consultant.

BISTRO COOKING
Anne Willan Founder and director of La Varenne Cookery School in Burgundy and West Virginia. Author of many books and a specialist in French cuisine.

ITALIAN COOKING
Anna Del Conte is the author of *The Classic Food of Northern Italy* (chosen as the 1996 Guild of Food Writers Book of the Year) and *The Gastronomy of Italy*. She has appeared on BBC-TV's *Masterchef*.

VIETNAMESE COOKING
Nicole Routhier One of the United States' most popular cookery writers, her books include *Cooking Under Wraps, Nicole Routhier's Fruit Cookbook* and the award-winning *The Foods of Vietnam*.

MALAYSIAN COOKING
Jill Dupleix One of Australia's best known cookery writers, with columns in the *Sydney Morning Herald* and *Elle*. Author of *New Food, Allegro al dente* and the Master Chefs *Pacific*.

PEKING CUISINE
Helen Chen Learned to cook traditional Peking dishes from her mother, Joyce Chen, the grande dame of Chinese cooking in the United States. The author of *Chinese Home Cooking*.

STIR FRIES
Kay Fairfax Author of several books, including *100 Great Stir-fries, Homemade* and *The Australian Christmas Book*.

NOODLES
Terry Durack Australia's most widely read restaurant critic and co-editor of the *Sydney Morning Herald Good Food Guide*. He is the author of *YUM!*, a book of stories and recipes.

NORTH INDIAN CURRIES
Pat Chapman Started the Curry Club in 1982. Appears regularly on television and radio and is the author of eighteen books, the latest being *The Thai Restaurant Cookbook*.

BARBECUES AND GRILLS
Brian Turner Chef/patron of Turner's in Knightsbridge and one of Britain's most popular food broadcasters; he appears frequently on *Ready Steady Cook, Food and Drink* and many other television programmes.

SUMMER AND WINTER CASSEROLES
Anton Edelmann Maître Chef des Cuisines at the Savoy Hotel, London, and author of six books. He appears regularly on BBC-TV's *Masterchef*.

TRADITIONAL PUDDINGS
Tessa Bramley Chef/patron of the acclaimed Old Vicarage restaurant in Ridgeway, Derbyshire. Author of *The Instinctive Cook*, and a regular presenter on a new Channel 4 daytime series *Here's One I Made Earlier*.

DECORATED CAKES
Jane Asher Author of several cookery books and a novel. She has also appeared in her own television series, *Jane Asher's Christmas* (1995).

FAVOURITE CAKES
Mary Berry One of Britain's leading cookery writers, her numerous books include *Mary Berry's Ultimate Cake Book*. She has made many television and radio appearances and is a regular contributor to cookery magazines.

First published in 1997 by
George Weidenfeld & Nicolson
The Orion Publishing Group
Orion House
5 Upper St Martin's Lane
London WC2H 9EA

British Library Cataloguing-in-Publication data
A catalogue record for this book is available from
the British Library

ISBN 0 297 82285 3

Designed by Lucy Holmes
Edited by Maggie Ramsay
Food styling by Joy Davies
Typeset by Tiger Typeset